The Paper Sky

The Paper Sky

El Gruer

CANTERBURY
PRESS
Norwich

First published in 2015 by the Canterbury Press Norwich
Editorial office
3rd Floor, Invicta House,
108–114 Golden Lane,
London EC1Y 0TG, UK

Canterbury Press is an imprint of Hymns Ancient & Modern Ltd
(a registered charity)
13A Hellesdon Park Road, Norwich,
Norfolk NR6 5DR, UK

www.canterburypress.co.uk

British Library Cataloguing in Publication data

A catalogue record for this book is available
from the British Library

978 1 84825 767 2

Typeset by Regent Typesetting
Printed and bound in Great Britain by
CPI Group (UK) Ltd, Croydon

Contents

For You,

With love

x

Hayley,
you are wonderful,
keep giving
life your whole heart!
With love
EL ☺

In the half-blink of morning,
I crawl to you in a whisper.

Preface

This collection was written from a heart longing to vocalise the breadth of human experience. These poems are a library of voices, both imagined and actual. Although none of these voices are explicitly mine, I am in all of them. I chose to step into the footsteps of the everyone and the no one.

Some of the longer poems are written for the stage and you may benefit from reading them aloud and some of the shortest can be used as meditations for the soul.

The Paper Sky also contains two series of poems that communicate a wider narrative, *When Leaves Fall* and *Becoming Lilian*.

I invite you into the raw space that all of these voices inhabit, in the hope that in experiencing others' heartbeats, we would also meet our own gaze. It is my prayer that you might find an echo of yourself; after all, in the silence after gunshots, we are all one.

In the gasps after tears drop, we are all one.
As the sky begins to fold, we are all one.

Paper Sky

As I drove, the radio sang
its own anger down the avenue.
I saw the rows of tightly sewn houses
like coppered Monopoly pieces,
end to end to end and
I wished that in these I saw my mind.
From the lead edging of the rooftops
there fluxed a ricochet of starlings and
I thought
       there, there and
I watched
       the twisting birds
              leak like ink onto the paper sky.

Hoods

I learnt not to care for Care
or dare to foster dreams.
There was a rhythm to my life –
Mum was the black, blue, beaten wife, sister took her
    own life.
Dad was all I had but alcohol had all of Dad,
so don't assume I care for Care or ever could.
I wear my lack of care for Care under my hoodie hood.

You'll find we all hide
under hoods of different kinds
and no matter what hood we're under,
we feel misunderstood.

I am a widow but you wouldn't know
as I pre-heat my smile for it not to show.
I knead my need to be needed into cookie dough.
I bake for neighbourhood luncheons, community functions,
    all occasions,
baking all butter scones and scones with raisins.
Since my partner passed I've masked the half-heartbeat of
    widowhood.
I wear my need to be needed under my cooker hood.

You'll find we all hide
under hoods of different kinds
and no matter what hood we're under,
we feel misunderstood.

I park my soft-top convertible outside the Spar
but I never made it as a sports star,
haven't owned a classy bar,
not rocked out on a stage guitar,
all my business plans never got very far.
Now I'm feeling trapped in an office job and charcoal suit
taking ready meals for one out of my fancy car boot.
I wear my mid-life crisis
under my convertible car hood.

You'll find we all hide
under hoods of different kinds
and no matter what hood we're under,
we feel misunderstood.

I am a mother of four you see,
now I dream in Lunchables of Dairylea,
holidays where kids go free,
I know every line from 'Toy Story 3',
I've perfected balancing four kids on two knees
but I wear my *help, somewhere I've lost me*,
under the busyness of motherhood.

You'll find we all hide
under hoods of different kinds
and no matter what hood we're under,
we feel misunderstood.

There's the likelihood
that if you Google *hood*,
the list will include
your hood or so it should.

Maybe it was being rude
in your childhood,
or a feud that tore a sisterhood.
Maybe it was a romance in your girlhood
or the bromance of a brotherhood.
Maybe you were named infertile by motherhood
or feel a failure in your fatherhood.

Perhaps you buried yourself in servanthood
or tried to fit in with the neighbourhood.
Maybe in your adulthood
you haven't experienced a spinsterhood
or dedicated to the priesthood
but at the very least
you should have a hood
as every person has
a personhood.

So whether you're on happy meals
or meals on wheels,
there's no need for me to remind –
you will find, we all hide
under hoods of different kinds
and no matter what hood we're under,
we feel misunderstood.

The Cousin-hood

You were tree sap that sticks between fingertips.
You were the giddy spin from a rope swing –
now hanging motion   l
                      e
                      s
                      s

in farmyard sweat.

I was the brand new wellingtons and the sandwich with
   no crust.

Abandoned in the   s t r e a m.

We wore grass for ankle socks, stretched sunlight into
   tree houses.
Nostrils delirious from dung, we were the smell of
   summer washing
now   b
       l
         o
       w
     n
       into the barbed wire of years.

You asked me
if I had seen love.
I replied, *I've seen the Ocean.*

When Leaves Fall

Winter

It was the first Saturday in December and our scattered
   cousinhood was neatly embroidered
back into Old Pa's front room.
And Old Pa
sagged in his corner chair, letting our youth-filled rabble
   banquet him
with Werthers and hot air stories.

My mother and her sisters childminded their mince pies by
   the Aga while the husbands
hoisted,
pruned,
and hoisted
a conifer into centre stage. This labour required a break

and this was our cue to begin ordaining the tree with a hoard
   of pre-loved tack
(which always takes the same divine order):

a long twist of coloured lights (usually at least three
   bulbs blown),
         coppery tinsel (fatigued gold),
            glassy baubles (with cataracts),
               candied canes (Aunt Mo's annual offering),
and a creep of genderless hanging elves.

(After which commenced the official interval)

En masse,
we unfoiled the perfection of mince pies and sipped warmed
    grape juice from plastic tumblers.
Little Lily nested with Old Pa, both drinking their mulled
    communion through straws.
During this interval,
there was a testosterone-centred discussion
on where the ladder for the attic was abandoned last year,
before Uncle Adam ascended (he is the least affected by dust)
    and returned carrying the Christmas box
like the Ark of the Covenant from the loft.

This year it was Robbie's turn to unfold Great Aunt Jennifer's
    angel (handmade)
from the crepe-paper.
I didn't know much about Great Aunt Jennifer,
although my first sister was named after her
(a stillborn: Jenny).

Robbie hoisted the angel's doily skirts and pedestaled her
onto the prickling of needles.
In the swell of after-applause, I caught the pale end of
    Lily's question
                'and why does the angel look so sad?'

Spring

Uncle Adam was on the patio, wafting an end of cardboard to
 light the charcoals.
Just pop the burgers there, he gestured to the table with the
 stack of neatly cut foil.

I crouched for Lily as she tugged my arm and whispered,
 this is you,
and opened her hand. There was a single acorn in the bowl of
 her palm.

I enlisted the twins to carry the wooden platters of salad
 covered with cling film
as I clutched an array of bottles – Pinot Grigio, sparkling
 water and a Chilean Merlot.

In the garden, I heard Robbie decline a taste of Uncle Derek's
 home-made gin,
Lily jumped from the swing as Dad announced the first round
 of sausages was cooked.

Mum fluttered a teal blanket onto the lawn by Old Pa's feet,
pinned the fringes of one end and secured it with two rocks
 and a cool box.

Our platters bowed in the centre as we jigsaw-pieced
 ourselves on the rug,
Robbie balanced his portion as he probed the ketchup bottle
 with a disposable knife.

Old Pa chased a rogue tomato around the ridging of his
    paper plate
as Aunt Mo overdosed Lily with mid-afternoon suncream.

I sat cross-legged, let my spine straighten
anchored by the acorn in my pocket.

Summer

Aunt Mo had left a note, *thanks for childminding*, with a
   batch of still-warm scones.
We bagged two and, holding hands, walked the towpath to
   the river.

As we sat on a bench, Lily operated, extracted every raisin
   from the scone
and slotted them individually into her mouth.

She carried the napkin, polka-dotted with crumbs, to
   the railings
and tipped them into the Lagan.

For the starlings, she commanded
to the ripple and swallow of the water.

Autumn

I was mid-meeting
when the phone rang
and fell to voicemail.

* * *

Before the next appointment,
I locked my office door,

listened to Mum's voice
strung thinly.

* * *

In the family room
on the children's ward,
we sat too far apart,
our bodies uninhabited.

The surgeon buffered
the door with his toe,
it closed softly.

* * *

I pulled into the short-stay bay,
waited to pick Robbie
up from the train:
the dark circles of our eyes met.

* * *

At the wake,
people were careful
not to bring lilies,

the canapés
remained uneaten.

* * *

For eight days,
the rain kept
its own vigil
as the carnations wilted.

We became the lament
of black umbrellas dripping
on linoleum.

* * *

After my first day back at work,
I met Old Pa's home-help
on his driveway. As she left,

she mouthed,
He's back on the cigarettes.

* * *

From the wordless stillness
of Old Pa's front room,
I popped to the farm
with enough clothes for a week.

Mum met me at the gate
with chicken feed in a pail.
Just an overnight, I said.
Her blanched face rosied.

* * *

I nodded to the vacant placemat,
Dad still working?

*He didn't come in for dinner
last night either.*

* * *

As I wiped a splattering of mushy peas
from the tablecloth, I pretended
not to see the tremor of Mum's shoulders

and the tears that dropped
into the soapy basin.

* * *

Her voice slipped to a lullaby
as she phoned Aunt Mo,

*Uhuh, I know, I know,
it'll all take time,
be patient with yourself,
uhuh, I know, I know.*

As the receiver clicked
I moved to the hallway,

and found Mum stabbing a block
of Post-it notes with a Bic.

* * *

At the dining table,
I swaddled myself
with a cerise blanket
and began to make
a bucket list
on the back of a receipt.

* * *

Just after nine o'clock,
Dad stomped the dirt
from his boots at the back door.

He hugged me with weighty arms,
his breath – a cocktail
of pig and whiskey.

* * *

I lay in the top bunk
of the room I had shared
with the twins,

stared into the yellowed
plastic stars on the ceiling

and focused on the escape of my breath.

* * *

On Saturday, I drove Mum to Aunt Mo's.
They sat in the conservatory,
recycling inhalations in unison.

Uncle Adam and I
climbed the stairs to Lily's room
with black bags.

Are you sure it's not too soon?
Mum's syllables slid up
the banister behind us.

* * *

Her school bag was resting
against the chest of drawers.
In the front pouch was a pencil,
a ruler and a rubber in the shape of a bird.

The pencil was pale blue,
half its original size and well chewed.
As Uncle Adam folded a pinafore,
I slid it up my sleeve.

* * *

It was the jotter,
holding the practice
of her joined-up writing,
that caught me.

I hung from the loop in her '*y*'s.

* * *

I looked at Uncle Adam
and gave a single shake of my head.

With the bin liners still on the roll,
and her clothes folded in rows,

we closed the door
and sealed the archive.

Winter

After work, I leant on the glossed railings and waited
for the dark swell of starlings.

* * *

From the Co-op, I bought a four-pack of fruit scones.

With my back against the eggshell blue wall,
I squatted on the floor
of my one-bed maisonette.

I broke the scones apart,
picked all the raisins out, set them on a tissue,
then ate them in one fistful,

leaving the crumbs as an offering on the rug.

Spring

We shuffled onto the slate steps at Old Pa's front door,
took our positions for the annual photograph.

Old Pa was centred as we symmetrically interspersed ourselves,
the twins bookending the middle row.

Uncle Adam propped the camera on the neighbour's wall
as he set up the self-timed snap.

I moved slightly in to half-fill a gap
and looked at the ticking light above the lens

watching it grow frantic
and then stop in a heartbeat.

The same sky
I look upon and pray,
you look to and cry.

The Cruellest Word in Mother-hood

Why couldn't it be
quiet-born or
tranquil-born?

I would even persuade myself
to endure *soundless-born,*
gone-born or *inactive-born*
and with a laborious push,
limp-born.

Still now, your form has been stamped
with teething syllables that contract.
Reminding me,
that whether you held breath in the space
called life or the space called death, after
nine months of mother-hood's baited breath
you were
still born.

A Lullabye

To my baby in the incubator,
love will always out-dream the night ghost.

There was news in the surgeon's eyes,

time had contracted,
his soul was birthed into eternity.

So I sing
to my infant, I sing
a lulla-bye.

Misconception

You started as a thin blue line

then nurse's hands and a scan
vocalised you as a healthy peanut,
a peanut with a breath-ready heartbeat
and a real kick.

Out of my body's shell
you were as dead as a peanut

salted in the wound.

I became days of fragile blue.

Homebirth

Tonight the sky seems heavier
like the daytime's
stillborn twin.
I think of the Chinese proverb,
women hold up half the sky,
and I conceive that the dead
hold up the rest.

The hours drip
and Mama sings
an inaudible lullaby
and cries blood
onto the kitchen table.
I am still holding a seeping cloth,
eyes pricking with Dettol and shock.

Greenhome

I asked to pay the gardener for her womb
as she was cutting back the mulberry bloom
that creeps up the garage wall.
I said I'd pay her well - a preening bonus.
I tried to seduce her with horticultural terminology –
grafting my stem to her plant,
produce sweetpeas to grow strong
in our greenhouse, greenhome.
She ignored me again
and continued hacking at the foliage,
thorns falling at my wellied feet.
I dismissed myself inside
and from the kitchen I watched
the curve of her hips like terracotta pots.
I resigned to doodling on my 'to do' list.
I am fifty and still childless.

April

It was the day we made plasticine models,
that I knew.
We sat in your parents' dining room,

the two of us, your brother and the little one.
April dripped from the eaves.
At the little one's command

we thumbed purple into figurines,
marched them in their pairs
towards the frame of a church.

You felt for my knee under the table.
I let you rest your palm there
while I rolled a miniature child

with the sticky remains.
I shaped her with a skirt,
two curled flicks for hair.

We haven't made any trees,
the little one said, as your brother
peeled a fresh green strip

of plasticine from the packaging.
April continued to drip.
We spend the afternoon creating trees,

placing our purple people
in a circle on the mahogany,
my tiny girl motionless in the middle.

The little one flattened the church,
formed an oversized picnic blanket,
laid it underneath the citizens

of our soggy afternoon.
Your hand had left my knee in the busyness
of crafting trees and I wanted to crawl

alone under the table and cry
with the tiny purple child
between my finger and thumb

but instead I looked towards
the heavy frame of the window
and watched the rain.

Venison Stew Recipe

I was perched on a high stool,
elbows propped on the kitchen island
blowing into a ceramic mug of tea.

My back was to the eco-wall of windows
that framed the late September trees
as my Godmother made a venison stew.

She relived a Rhodesian childhood
as she diced the rump meat, recalling
the mid-June song of the buttonquail

courting in the warming grasses –
the *hoom – hoom – hoom* of the female,
the *kek – kek – kek* of her mate.

Her bird notes were softly punctuated
with the opening of cupboard doors
and the *hum-click* as the fridge closed.

In a clay pestle and mortar
she crushed ripe juniper berries
mouthing the word *refugee*

at eighteen and in early January
through home forests of flame lilies
she tip-toed twelve borders

to meet promised asylum in Turkey.
She paused as she checked potatoes
then added a rosemary stem to the stock.

She lamented her accent now diluted
with forty years of Scottish land, pines
and the footprints of red grouse.

I placed the empty mug on the counter
and moved to the cutlery drawer
through the *trill – trill – trill* of local game.

She raised a serving spoon to her lips,
dusted seasoning then tasted again
as I set placemats on the oak table.

She ladled the marinated stories
of our supper into terracotta bowls
crowning them with steamed greens.

Our main course budded into the current
climate – its rare afternoon sightings
of the yellow shell moth.

For our dessert she sketched
bluebells, cloudberries and the silhouette
of the common bell-heather.

Scars tell stories,
rich stories,
of tissue healed.

I asked for bread.
You opened your hand
and gave me a nest.

The Robin

It was the day we created the snowman
that I made the decision.

We stood in your parents' back garden,
the two of us, your brother and the little one.

We were knee deep in December,
the birches bare and frail,

the robin only appearing at noon
when your mother scattered seeds.

I had cried in the shower that morning
while you were stifled mid-snore.

Now as the little one burrowed
stone eyes into the snowman's face

I wanted to crawl into the spare corners
of winter but instead I placed

the carrot for the nose and commented
on the brightness of the scarf.

The Half of It

Words had expired so we used eyes
and a horse's soul
to talk about forbidden things. Unlike the unflinching words,
eyes could not be regret.

Words had expired so we used trees
and an upturned boat
to talk about our appetite. Unlike the irrigated words,
trees could not be war.

Words had expired so we used chairs
and polystyrene cups
to talk about our future. Unlike the infidelity of words
chairs could not be misread.

Words had expired so we used concrete
and pigeon feathers
to talk about our children. Unlike the illness of words
concrete could not be a nest.

Trafficked

What people do is not so far apart
from the condition of their heart.

From this ordeal what I have come to find
is that bound people bind people,
captive people capture people,
sold people sell people,
caged people cage people,
damaged people damage people,
enslaved people enslave people
because hurt people hurt people.

What people do is not so far apart
from the condition of their heart.

From this ordeal what I choose to remind people
is that found people find people,
restored people restore people,
honoured people honour people,
loved people love people,
redeemed people redeem people,
healed people heal people,
hope-filled people fill hope in people
because free people free people.

What people do is not so far apart
from the condition of their heart.

Unfortunately it seems
the abusers are the relentless   relentless   relentless
not those trying to save us   save us   save us.

If those fighting against this
had the same persistence, in this instance
it would have made all the difference.

Caged people don't think twice about caging people
and the free people don't believe it's their place to free people.
We're left with a lot of humanity in all types of outrageous cages
calling out desperately   desperately   desperately to be heard –
freedom needs to be more than a word.

From this ordeal this is my very real plea

free people   please free people.

Rwanda 1994

Forget your crying, child, for the sky has heard it all before.

Now, in old Meme's harsh words, I found a lullaby –
there was, at least
one witness

        who heard me die.

Svay Pak, Cambodia 2013

At seven, I was sketching
hopscotch with chalk
on the cul-de-sac paving
giggle.skip.giddy.hop.giggle.skip.giddy.hop

young girls playing in pinafores,
laughing through knees grazing on tarmac,
slipping shoes off at the back door.

                    Mealea was six thousand miles' worth
                         of different child, Cambodian dirt
                              in every orifice
         raped.night.raped.day.raped.night.raped.day

                    grown men playing, post-genocide,
         girls locked in cells with bloodied mattresses
                         and half a cup of rice.

    Now we look at each other,
    ripe women
    sitting cross-legged in the rainy season
    our ages even and fifteen years on.

    Washing is slung along corrugated
    sheets through openings in the slum.
    She threads a ruby bead onto a bracelet
    that later becomes the parting gift.

Her ten years of torture are spoken
into the nutshell of ten minutes,
a few hand gestures
and a translator's pigeon English.

I watch the flies descend on the bowl
of rice and beans between us.
In the emptiness of her eyes
I swallow.I drown.I drown.I drown.I drown.

Gardening Tools 1988

I am kneeling in the garden
of a restoration centre,
Phnom Penh, Cambodia.

Propped up at the raised bed
there is a hoe, a fork,
a rake and two spades.

With one glance
at their sharpened edges
I am unravelled to ten years ago.

The native sky is entrenched
in a post-midnight blackout.
I am eight and huddled,

my skin dried across my bones
with other once-children
in a redundant rice field.

I know Mama is third
from the left in the line-up
of shadow-bodies

kneeling in the mud,
facing a pit, blood's steam
hissing into the dusk.

Through the crackling
tannoy, they played
propaganda music

which swallowed the cries
but between faints
of consciousness

I saw him –
the soldier with the spade
he was a little taller

but about my age.
He aligned the shovel
to the peak of her spine

took a weighty swing,
let its curse fall accurately.
I must have convulsed

involuntarily, for the soldier
guarding our child-nest
of skeletals, gripped his rake

and watched me watch
as Mama's mouth formed
a gaping O.

Now, some nights
I see it as a black hole,
that hollowed O,

in other flashbacks
it is my panicked gasp.
Last winter

I remembered it
as her grasping
for my name.

Describe to me the Post-war

This is how it will be (a trinity of scenes).
Scene one is the re-entrance.
We will play our own parts, giving time to our characters.
I will be reclined, wrapped in a damson throw,
draped across the window chair.
There will be a crumpled newspaper napping
beside an afternoon coffee cup. (You enter)
You will bring in the fresh scent of chopped wood.
The kindling will splinter to the carpet as we re-kindle fire
    that the enemy stole.
With a new season on our lips we will rejoice reunion in
    each other.
And it will be as if there was no war. Almost.

Scene two is the re-awakening.
When you awaken you will find me on the dock
dripping my feet in the morning chill,
the peel of an orange still between my fingertips.
We will spend sunrise gazing into the eyes of the lake.
Out with words you will hold me.
Moments that the enemy stole will be re-born in us.
With a new season in our eyes, we see images of truth in
    each other.
And it will be as if there was no war. Almost.

Scene three is the re-dreaming.
As time begins to darken,
we will spend days in the sigh of a wicker chair.
With creators' hands we will trace promises on each
other's faces.
With eternal bread that the enemy could not steal,
we will entertain angels as dinner guests.
With a new season in our hearts we will memorise the word
future in each other.
And it will be as if there was no war. Almost.

Eating Ate Away at Me

Its starter was my mind.
It fed me snack-size lies about my size
which distorted my inner eyes.
It showed me other parts of my life that lay in crumbs,
it made its domain in my brain and before I knew it
I was passing all my meal choices through its voice
and it was calculated in over-calculating calories.
It didn't ask if I minded it invading my mind,
it just moved in.
My mind was its first victim.

Its greed made it want to feed on all the more of me.
Of course, its main course was my body.
It ran circles round my square meals.
It got silently stronger
while I got silently weaker,
my hair became lank
as it drank the rosiness from my skin.
It sat back and saw success in my disintegrating,
while success for me was when I went to bed hungry.
It convinced me I was in control of it,
the dull ache in my gut actually made me smile
but all the while, eating ate away at me
as Anorexia made a three-course meal of me.
My body was its second victim.

Its dessert was my soul.
It was so bold it took a bite out of who I was
It took my focus away from wholeness.
People told me *to treat myself well*
but that felt closer to hell than help.

Any kind of nourishment translated into discouragement.
Self-compassion is not in fashion,
for me, it chose self-punishment.
My soul was its third victim.

Eating ate away at me as
Anorexia made a meal of me.
Mind, body and soul,
its three-course meal that left me hollow.

It chewed my ability to live freely,
it ate my creativity,
nibbled my sociability, my intimacy,
it digested the very essence of me.
My whole identity it swallowed whole.
It engorged my enjoyment,
threatened my employment and
relished the rest of my flesh.

But Anorexia's cutlery will no longer cut away at me.
I have given myself to a creative nutrition
which restores the nervous system and
helps my ears to listen.
I gave my soul into the bold hold of self-trust
to dust away the distasteful taste of wasting away.

Anorexia, you may have run circles round my square meals
but I look at you squarely, telling you to circle this
I AM FREE.
You cannot count the calories on my colour palette.

Eating, for a time
you made a meal of me
but now my mind is a field where wild flowers grow,
my body is a beating heart without walls
and my soul is a banquet of creativity.

A Fix of Addiction

You think it might be ordinary
to start the day with a bowl of Special K.
But it's not so ok
when one bowl of Sugar Puffs isn't enough
and you start to lust after Honey Nut Clusters.

I began to notice withdrawal symptoms.
When I had the mid-morning shakes,
I knew I needed a hit of Bran Flakes.
If my right eye started to twitch
that signalled the need for Weetabix.
If it was a left eye twitch, it meant Oatibix.
If both eyes were twitching and then started itching,
then I needed a mix of the bixs.

Addiction can be stranger than fiction
but it's a very real affliction.
The thing about addiction
is that addiction is addiction.
Your mind becomes transfixed
on where your next fix is from.
The irony is, it's not fixing anyone.
What's depressing is you're just suppressing
what you really should be wrestling with.

A rough day drives some to cheap cider
but I drowned my sorrows in Fruit and Fibre.
I'm not one to go out drinking
but I stayed in and got emotionally wrecked on Ready Brek.

You won't be shocked to know
that I stopped shopping in shops
that weren't well stocked with Coco Pops and Coco Rocks.
I didn't go to bed with the comfort of teddies,
I sleep soundly snuggling a box of Shreddies.
Marbles? I had totally lost these!
I dreamt unashamedly in Frosties.
But it's costly (not just 'cos cereal is extensively expensive),
it cost me my sanity, exposing me
as a complete Fruit Loop.

The thing about addiction
is that addiction is addiction.
Your mind becomes transfixed
on where your next fix is from.
The irony is, it's not fixing anyone.
What's depressing is you're just suppressing
what you really should be wrestling with.

As the addiction deepened, it infiltrated my brain
and I started to experiment with Nutri-grains.
I'd be looking over my shoulder,
afraid if sniffer dogs sniffed me,
they'd find pockets filled with Rice Crispies.
My friends were going out for social pub meals.
The only social place I went to was the Special K bar.
I knew it had gone too far,
when I went for coffee with a friend.
She said, *You look distant.*
I said, *I'm just thinking.*
Oh, what's his name?
She mistook the clouds in my eyes,
for the presence of a guy.
I said, *Graham*, which wasn't a lie.
I couldn't wait for my next date with Cinnamon Grahams.

I knew I had hit an all-time low
when fighting defeat
required me to repeat
No, No, No to a box of Raisin Wheats,
and Pomegranate Wheats, and Apricot Wheats and
    Raspberry Wheats
No.No.No

But it just goes to show,
addiction causes great harm
and I'm not just talking about
the sugar content in Lucky Charms.
The thing about addiction
is that addiction is addiction.
Your mind becomes transfixed
on where your next fix is from.
The irony is, it's not fixing anyone.
What's depressing is you're just suppressing
what you really should be wrestling with.

It doesn't need to be heroin,
for us to be inherently in too deep.
You need to remind your mind that
there is more to life than this.

Addiction is the opposite of enriching,
it snorts a hole in your soul,
leaves you totally un-whole,
unfixed,
in a hole,
in a fix.

So I took a clean break from Corn Flakes,
abandoned my plan to find comfort in All Bran.
My life will not succumb to the pitter-patter
downward pattern of addiction.

Crunchy Nut, you did nothing but bruise me.
Alpen, you did nothing but use me.
Granola, you did nothing but abuse me.
Muesli, you no longer amuse me.
I said cheerio to Cheerios
and chose to lose my taste for cereals.

You needed to remind my mind
that there was more to life than this.
Addiction's a curse, freedom's a kiss
but this means wrestling
with what you've been suppressing
which as you are guessing,
isn't easy but it frees you.

The thing about addiction
is that addiction is addiction.
Your mind becomes transfixed
on where your next fix is from.
The irony is, it's not fixing anyone.
What's depressing is you're just suppressing
what you really should be wrestling with.

Chopping

You were chopping dates when I said it – it leaked from me
                  and it took us back 8 years and 400 miles
to where it was buried.
        I could taste soil under my tongue as you now paused,
the little blue Ikea knife raised,
              the dates abandoned.

The words formed worms between us,
                compost shifted into sick and I tasted it.
You turned on your heel too calmly
           your Catholic eyes asking if this was necessary.

You were chopping dates when I said it – I tried to catch
   the syllables
but they reeled out
             and it took us back 8 years and 400 miles.

Anniversary

Once eight o'clock had ticked and gone
she ate a bowl of Bolognese, three flapjacks,
a Jaffa Cake and twelve grapes.
She drummed her fingers on the kitchen table,
slopped Merlot into a gold-rimmed glass
then paced, sipped, paced, sipped, paced,
slippers tapping on linoleum.

He clicked the key into the Yale
and met the dank breath
you said you'd be home at six
as she hurled the pan of spaghetti
at the ceiling.
The pasta stuck, hanging between them
tentacles dripping.

Arcades

You were nineteen and between jobs,
sleeping in our front room – my brother owed you one.

I was fourteen and pretending to be vegan,
spending Easter creating découpage from recycling.

On the last Saturday of April, I followed you
and a Sainsbury's bag of coppers to the arcades

on Brighton pier. Angled to the slot, you emptied yourself
in penny after penny after penny after penny.

With your winnings you had said you'd bargain me
    a Dachshund
but you returned with a bratwurst from the burger van.

The pulse of the arcades – men bowed and frantic
gave me the designs for an art installation.

I spent the evening pencilling a slot machine
swollen with hotdogs and titled it *Testosterone*.

By mid-May you were gone, I sketched the bonsai tree
    you left
while Mum Febreezed the couch.

Afternoon Tea for One

I find myself as a shadow
in the cheap upstairs cafe
making a scone of us.

I looked at it lying lifeless
on the clinical plate – separated
in unequal halves.
I let the mirroring knife
slide across the softening marg
and I remembered
how you had buttered me up.

I find myself as a shadow
in the old upstairs cafe
digesting a scone of us.

I eat the smaller half and wrap
your side in a crumbed serviette.
I take the usual route back
through town to the cul-de-sac.
As I pass the *Big Issue* man
in Derek's Chippie doorway
I see your vacancy in his eyes.

I find myself as a shadow
pausing in stale air
giving away a scone of us.

On Writing Love

I can no longer plot stars into constellations
or borrow a sun for the sky.

I cannot allow quilt squares to be sewn together
or let fresh sheets make beds.

I cannot consider hinging doors into terracotta frames
or see through the pane of windows.

I can never set the sail of boats onto the sea,
or let Autumn escort Summer.

I have learnt too much of love
to write life into its earthly place.

Notes Found in a Trench

(i)
The world was an oyster in the palm
of my hand.
As one of the boys I marched
into the army. As pretend men
we traded our oysters for the glint of bullets.
My frontline trigger finger was locked
in automatic, firing men's souls
into harrowed soil.
My oyster recoiled into a trench of
narrowed eyes and last gasps.

As a hollowed man I stagger,
all I am is the dull clinking
of bullets in a hand.

(ii)
Dear Daddy,
                    I tried to post myself to you. I thought I bought
enough stamps. I wore brown like brown paper. I thought
we could go to the seaside. I stood beside the pillar box.
The postman said he couldn't deliver me to you. Tomorrow
I will try again and I'll make a passport, maybe I should fly.
Does 'Frontline' have an airport?   Love Elsie xx

(iii)
War had no right,
just a left,
it left the shells
of hollowed men.

Artism

They said I should add it to my routine chart
they said I should see art – have art in my day.
I think it was because they were at
the end of a thing they call a *tether*.
They took me to a space called *gallery*
to look at art – have art in my day.
I showed them this face ☺

I didn't see any art. I saw a lot of mess.
There were ketchup explosions on canvas.
There was too much blue.
My head went for a swim.
I showed them this face ☹
I think they were at the place
called a tether again because they didn't have
happy on their faces.

They asked me what art I would
like to look at – have in my day?
I said, *I already have art.*
I said, *I am art.* Because I am.
I breathe. I walk. I talk. I sleep. I am.
I am autistic and I am a work of art.

Inheritance

The study seemed to yawn
with the debris of stacked books
and maps stretched across the carpet.
Aunt Debbie thumbed the set of pearls
that lay opened on the sideboard.
Uncle Tom smiled from the corner chair
and passed around a photograph
of Grandma caught mid-laugh.

I'll put the kettle on, I spoke
as Mum propped the window open
with a wearied 'Wuthering Heights'.
In the back kitchen, I smiled
at the familiar blue-glazed pot
and its nest of utensils.

As the teapot warmed
I lifted out the red-handled spatula –
the one Grandma always used to coax
scrambling eggs from a greasy pan
onto my Sunday plate.
Hearing the veil of distant laughter
I held the spatula up to my chest
and then slid it into my jacket pocket.

The Lemon Drizzle Love Song

Well-meaning people like to throw me pity parties
saying, *it must be hard for your heart
to know such aloneness* (like it was a bitter taste).
It's been so long since you have even had a date!
I felt the need to explain it, so their brains could retain it,
that I am willing to wait.
My love, we haven't met yet but I know it won't be long
so I wrote you a Lemon Drizzle Love Song,
showing that something they perceive to be so bitter,
I will receive as something so sweet.

This is the recipe of our romance
that will make our love like a Lemon Drizzle cake.
You will take the first step and risk to *whisk* me away.
You'll bring *flour*(s), *egg*sactly as it should be.
You won't try to butter me up,
knowing that I won't sponge from you.
We'll be the zest we've ever met.
Synchronising in our rising,
the timing of us will be the icing of us,
generously drizzled, we will not fizzle out.
We will have a rich consistency
because love enlisted this recipe.

I don't know who we are but I know what we are not.
We are not a shop-bought lemon compote,
we are not a gooey in a tub lemon syllabub,
we are not a hard-based factory fake taste lemon cheesecake,
we are not a melt on a heated day lemon sorbet,
we are not a flat in the pan lemon flan,

we are not a showy Marks and Spencer sort of lemon torte,
we are not the dry puff of lemon meringue pie,
we're the real stuff you and I,
why?
Because our Lemon Drizzle Love is from above.

You'll confess the times that you lusted for lemon tarts
that you trusted and they broke your heart.
I'll forgive this, for in forgiveness we remove the bitterness
and taste the sweetness.
I'll tell you about that thing that was more of a cheap fling
with that Mr Kipling.
You'll forgive this, for in forgiveness we remove the bitterness
and taste the sweetness.

If we start to go stale, we won't fight
over who was meant to keep us airtight.
Going a little stale isn't wrong,
it's just another verse in the Lemon Drizzle Love Song.

I don't know who we are but I know what we are not.
We are not a shop-bought lemon compote,
we are not a gooey in a tub lemon syllabub,
we are not a hard-based factory fake taste lemon cheesecake,
we are not a melt on a heated day lemon sorbet,
we are not a flat in the pan lemon flan,
we are not a showy Marks and Spencer sort of lemon torte,
we are not the dry puff of lemon meringue pie,
we're the real stuff you and I,
why?
Because our Lemon Drizzle Love is from above.

We are made with real lemon peel,
a handmade, God-ordained,
full flavoured Lemon Drizzle cake
which gives the rich consistency to resist defeat.

Our love might be a little rough round the edges
but you can cut a big wedge from us
and there is enough for everyone.
Our love is so over the brim
that we don't fit in your average cake tin.

So pity party people, it may be a long time
since I even had a date
but pity party people
this is why I am willing to wait.
Something you perceive to be so bitter,
I will receive as something so sweet.
My love, until we meet
I'll put the Lemon Drizzle Love Song on repeat.

I don't know who we are but I know what we are not.
We are not a shop-bought lemon compote,
we are not a gooey in a tub lemon syllabub,
we are not a hard-based factory fake taste lemon cheesecake,
we are not a melt on a heated day lemon sorbet,
we are not a flat in the pan lemon flan,
we are not a showy Marks and Spencer sort of lemon torte,
we are not the dry puff of lemon meringue pie,
we're the real stuff you and I
why?
Because our Lemon Drizzle Love is from above.

Genealogies

On a bench on Brighton promenade I read our genealogies
while you were a silhouette at the water line
peppering stones into the sea.

My family tree stands in the furrows of a tattie field
dimpled with bullet wounds, whisky stains
and the rugged bark of Hectors, Rabs and Malcolms.

Yours has grown secure in the orchard of manor gardens
punctuated with inventors, Oxford PhDs
and the eloquence of Tarquins, Ruperts and Edwins.

I pinned our lineage under an ice cream tub and neon spoon
letting them converse in the breeze
while we ran barefoot, meeting halfway on the shingle.

The Wedding

At sixteen she married her childhood sweetheart,
who was wed to Leukaemia
and the squeal of the hospital bed.
They wrote their own vows,
knowing death would do them, apart.
One ceremony too early,
her grandmother wore black
but she affirmed the register,
looping her l's to loyalty
and dabbing her i's with intimacy.
That night they folded into each other
across porcelain sheets.
As lovers and determined youth,
they held each other into the clutch of death.
She was a widow at seventeen.

Crosswords

My grandparents always have cross words
laid out between them

One Across   Two Down
A vow broken   *Words unspoken*

They sit, sipping
from chipped-shoulder porcelain,
with nobody

filling in the blanks.

Hospital Bed – A week in the Death of

Monday
My eyes holiday upon the ocean. Through the ebb of hours,
I am a voyeur to the intimacy of wave on sand.

Tuesday
A kiss, a pull, a retract, a residue.
I can taste a faint perfume of shrivelling grapes and you.

Wednesday
Ears fill with the clinical tick of the slowing clock.
I drift to the maternal hum of machines.

Thursday
The hand that is still anchored to feeling
is holding a rich tapestry of nothingness.

Friday
I am a bride. I see a veil. Bells.
I trust this.

Saturday
Transcend
                    ascend

Sunday.

The Log Cabin

It is Autumn here – the trees are graduating into the crisp of
ochre. I am standing in the oak porch watching the halogen
moon age into the evening. I fill my lungs with the September
breeze and I know it is 1962. I have lit four cinnamon candles
on the mantel and seasoned the beef stew. When you come
home, I will tell you about my day, show you the pine cones I
dipped in gold enamel and strung above our bed.

I feel a tender press on my palm
I advance into my eyes.
There is an elderly man
  who looks like your grandfather but with slightly more hair,
                holding my hand.
I am in a single bed   it is not our bed
                no gold-dipped cones.
I can feel my eyes opening, widening
                     vaults into my head
my breath hurries out of me
            I clutch for air
                  but it is polystyrene.

The elderly man
whispers,   his voice like leaf

Go to the log cabin, Lily
            he holds the *y* into a breath like you do.

Elderly should be Senile and not Heard

I woke up this morning, my bed wasn't there,
again. I went to the bathroom and the toilet wasn't.
There were seven holes in the wall, again
I peed behind the sink, washed my hands on my face,
ate my wedding ring for breakfast.

I sat melting the rug with sparks
from my jewellery box,
coloured my toenails with a hairpin,
tore Revelation out of the Gideons,
and stuck it to my door with tree sap from my ear.

Interrupted, a lady in white
sang in a crisp 'Crimewatch' voice
Your daughter is here to see you.
I don't have children.
I showed her by stabbing my womb with an orange Smartie.

She put a chair underneath me,
made tea, watched 'til I drank it
with her and this false-claiming daughter
whose voice smelt of marigold
laced with Earl Grey.

I pretended to look at her but I
was looking past her
at my bed, pinned vertically
to the jasmine white emulsion wall
by four magpies and a puffin.

This daughter stayed
'til I had finished drinking my memory from a mug.
She patted my arm with a *bye Mum*.
I said nothing, it was another of their tests –
monitoring reactions. I triggered a smile to snap at her fringe.

If I passed this test I might get my toilet back,
maybe even my gun
to shoot the puffin.

Moments fold
into a chrysalis of days.
Breathe. Deep.
Light fades.

Milk Bottle Memory

They were glass, you remember,
with a foil lid and thumb dimple?
She speaks cautiously into the half-light
of present-past and Alzheimer's.

I breathe into a memory of milk bottles
and how they used to be delivered,
almost spiritually, to our top step.

And the boy, you remember, the boy?
her words create a concrete mind map
but I haze into watching the girl of me –
my chubby fingers grazed the upstairs curtains,
eyes locked on the milkman's boy
as he walked our unpaved path.
I listened for the soft *chink* and held my breath until
I heard the truck journey him away.
My slippered feet padded down the childhood staircase.
I wrapped my hands around the wintered bottles,
believing through some divine osmosis
that I could feel the warmth from his printed spirals.
Before the sibling clatter woke,
I poured the milk as a prayer on my cereal.

Yes, I remember, we called him Milky, is all I say.
Yes, Milky, she folds calmly, closing cataracts
into an afternoon sleep.

I sit at her bedside and waver
in the half-rise of an unpredicted blush.
We called him Milky, I whisper again,
tasting the white syllables of his name.

Becoming Lilian

There was a phone call,

was all my husband said
and I knew that, although
it had only been three weeks
since I saw my mother last,

she was now too far camouflaged.

* * *

On four trains I kept my luggage close,
thinking of the glass milk bottle
in bubblewrap.

* * *

After five hours, I was three hundred miles
from the emptiness of my empty nest.

* * *

For the first time in two years,
recognition blushed my mother's cheeks.

Lilian!

* * *

(Lilian had been her childhood friend)

I'm so glad you're here.

I think I am an orphan.

* * *

I unpacked the shopping
I'd picked up
and found the freezer crammed
with neapolitan ice-cream.

* * *

Today I woke up as Lilian.
At 6am, I joined my mother,

kneeling in the flowerbed
with a soiled nightie,

planting Fuchsia seeds.

* * *

Once I stopped resisting,
the transition to Lilian
was easy –
I ate fig rolls
and dropped myself
into a softer voice.

* * *

My mother, who raved about the nourishment
of milky porridge and dates,
asked for chocolate spread
and a fork.

* * *

She sat at the kitchen table
with a pencil, scratching illegible lines.

I must not forget my homework.
I must not forget my homework.

* * *

Crumpled behind a stack of Tupperware,
I found old jam labels
with my mother's handwriting.

I cried, holding them to my chest
as I lay, curled to an embryo
in the guest room.

* * *

The table was set for four,
I asked politely if we were expecting company?

Oh yes, did I forget to say?
The sparrows will be joining us
and they are never late.

* * *

The sparrows were prompt,
their company filled the kitchen.

My mother's eyes sank:
they left before dessert,
in a wingbeat.

* * *

I read three pages
of 'Anne of Green Gables' aloud
then set the ragged copy on the dresser.

She whispered, *let's say our prayers.*
I sat on the side of the bed
that my mother was tucked into.

I listened as she thanked God
for the day, asked for safety
as we slept.

Amen.

* * *

When my husband phoned,
I took a moment to get in character:

remembering to ask
about the dog, his work
and what he made for dinner.

When he asked about my mother,
all I could say was,
she is eleven and playing in the garden.

And are you still Lilian?
The question hung as pity between us.
Yes, I am Lilian, I replied, feeling defensive.

I am Lilian.

* * *

I tiptoed to the kitchen,
decanted milk from the carton
into the glass bottle I'd brought
and crowned it with a small disc of foil.

* * *

At 5am, I found the fridge door open.
My mother was sitting cross-legged
by the empty fireside
with a blue straw in the milk bottle,
blowing bubbles.

* * *

I can't find my school uniform.

It's the holidays, I said
and my mother skipped out
to make a daisy chain.

* * *

After lunch, I taught her how to make
Miracle Pudding,
which had been her signature dessert.
She slowly sifted self-raising flour
as I melted brown sugar and marg.

We both sat on the linoleum,
observed the gradual bubbling
through the oven's transparent panel,
watched it rise to the sharp beeping

of the egg-timer.

* * *

After my mother had gone to bed,
I crouched by the vacant fireside,
cradled the baking tray
and finished the pudding
with a teaspoon.

* * *

My husband phoned.
He had found a care home
we could afford, *not too far away
and with a garden.*

* * *

I delayed the moving date:
the sun was too generous
to keep her inside
and Lilian still had things to learn
about Geraniums.

* * *

When I took her to the home,
I told her we were going
to pick bluebells.

On the back seat
was the small tweed suitcase
of my mother's clothes,
disguised beneath a picnic blanket.

As I drove, the lie tasted
of foxglove.

Sunday Liturgy

I read the *Independent* in Starbucks
as I cupped an English Breakfast tea,

weaved through the black and white continents,
settling with the Congolese article.

Confessions of the Weapon of Rape,
Twelve Year Old Girls Hanging From Trees.

I followed Google Maps to St Peter's,
letting tears slip as I sang,

unsure whether I was crying
for the girls, my mother or Lilian,

but in worship I raised my hands,
stained with soil and newsprint.

Three Red Carnations

In the early afternoon, I took the coastal path into town,

bought a wicker garden basket
and threaded a Poundstretcher sunflower
through its weave.

My mind remained at my mother's with the
    half-packed boxes.

I indulged in a brownie
and a loose leaf tea on the balcony
of the corner coffee shop.

There were three red carnations in a jam jar on the glossed
    table top.

On my way home, I stopped,
sat on a peeling bench and watched
seagulls scuffle over breadcrumbs

and prayed a monologue into the lapping of the North Sea.

I wear on my sleeve, in blood,
this morning, I was given a rose,
a king that rose.

Sunday School

At five, I heard the name *Jesus*
and it echoed down my spine.

I wanted to run across wildflower fields,
bring him bold poppies I'd collected.

But instead, we had to sit cross-legged
under fluorescent strip lighting

and if we listened obediently, we'd sip
sickly diluting juice, feeling polystyrene on our lips.

Author

Author of old chapters,
with your touch,
turn these sepia pages,
turn my brokenness into a battle cry.

Author of new chapters,
with your touch,
turn these anticipated pages,
turn my brokenness into a battle cry.

Author of all chapters,
with your touch,
let me see your handwriting
all over my life.

I'm Sorry, Japan

In our world, it was one of those days.
I had to study for an exam so I didn't fail,
had a phone call with my Uncle Dale,
and it was *buy one get one free* at the picture sale.

It was there that I heard, Japan, you hit 9 on the Richter scale.
So I stopped. I thought.
I'm sorry, Japan.

I put my hair up into a ponytail
and put make-up on 'cos I was looking pale.
I booked a train with the national rail,
then opened bill, bill, bill and the rest of the mail.

Then I remembered, Japan, you hit 9 on the Richter scale.
I stopped. I thought.
I'm sorry, Japan.

But I had to get the washing in 'cos it was blowing a gale,
advise my best friend on her wedding veil
and pick up some shopping for Granny
as she's getting frail.

Then I remembered, Japan, you hit 9 on the Richter scale.
I stopped. I thought.
I'm sorry, Japan.

But by that time, the day was done
and the news was on.
From a comfortable distance,
I watched the day in your world.

I watched with eyes
desensitised to the perspective
of our Father's eyes because
I was tuned out from your
blood   spilt   cries.
I sat calmly, as your
flood-damaged   souls   died.
I stopped. I really thought.

I am sorry, Japan, that your earthquake
failed to shake me
to my knees to cry out
Father, *please, relieve.*

I am sorry, Japan,
that in my world, your world
wasn't a part of our world, didn't move
me to move things in the spiritual world.

I am sorry, Japan, that
as water filled 20,000 sets of lungs,
I was too busy to really stop and pray
for a
single
one.

I'm sorry, Japan,
that it wasn't my plan
to pray for you today.

Acorn

Take the acorn in my hand,
all I have,
and grow a mighty oak with it.

You are the artist of the acorn,
the sculptor of growth,
the architect of the oak.

I will praise you in the planting,
planting my worship. I will
worship you in the growing pains,
growing my adoration and
as an oak, I will adore you.

Take the acorn, all I am,
in your hand
and grow a rooted oak with it.

Weeping birds, don't cry
faithfulness is not a lie,
there is a tree
from which broken wings can fly.

God in a Box

When I take forward steps
I bubblewrap you into a removal box.

When I am feeling nostalgic
I fold you into a memoir box.

When I hear the echoes of my solitude
I dial you from a phone box.

When I feel the tug of sharing
I ribbon you into a gift box.

When my tears cry for comfort
I peel you from a tissue box.

When I remember your promises
I adorn you from a jewellery box.

When I am stale of passion
I spark you from a match box.

Oh, un-compartmentalisable God –
disturb our heads
with the explosive symphony
of bursting boxes.

Decompose our self plaster-casted pasts,
baptise our minds in your vastness.